SHHHH!!

Miriam, the baby and the secret basket boat

Bob Hartman

Illustrations by Emma Hagan

CWR

For Meili

Copyright © Bob Hartman 2014

Published 2015 by CWR, Waverley Abbey House, Waverley Lane, Farnham, Surrey GU9 8EP, UK.

CWR is a Registered Charity – Number 294387 and a Limited Company registered in England – Registration Number 1990308.

The right of Bob Hartman to be identified as the author of this work has been asserted by him
in accordance with the Copyright, Designs and Patents Act 1988 sections 77 and 78.

Visit www.cwr.org.uk/distributors for a list of National Distributors.

Concept development, editing, design and production by CWR.

Illustrations by Emma Hagan, visit www.emmahagan.co.uk

Printed in the UK by Linney Group

ISBN: 978-1-78259-360-7

This story is found in
Exodus 2–15

SHHH! My baby brother's asleep.

And, trust me,

you don't want to

wake him up.

He's really noisy!

Where is he?

If you promise
not to tell,
I'll show you.

Tell who?
Pharaoh,
of course.

Haven't you heard?

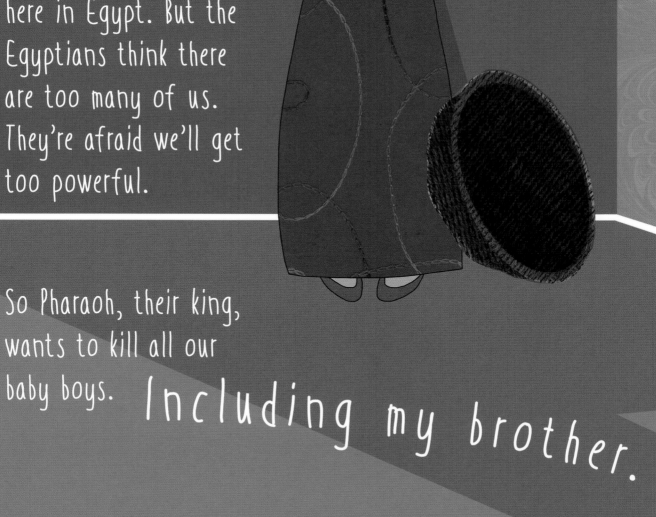

Hebrews, like me and my brother, we're slaves here in Egypt. But the Egyptians think there are too many of us. They're afraid we'll get too powerful.

So Pharaoh, their king, wants to kill all our baby boys. Including my brother.

Okay then, there he is,
sleeping in my mum's arms.
She's hiding him in the reeds
at the edge of the river –
in the bulrush basket she made for him.

What? All right, then.
Just a quick look.

He's beautiful, isn't he?

I sing to him sometimes.
This song my mum
taught me.

The Lord is my strength and my song

And He has become my salvation.

A strange song for slaves to sing, I know,
but ... wait, did you hear that?
Someone's coming. Better hide.
Look, it's some Egyptian ladies.
They've come down to the river to bathe, and ...

oh no!

They're pointing.
They're coming this way.
They've found the basket.
They're picking up my baby brother.

I can't look.

You are never going to believe this!

The woman who found my brother is one of Pharaoh's daughters.

She doesn't want to hurt him, she wants to **keep him!**

And she wants me to find a Hebrew woman to help raise him.

So I'm off to fetch my mum.

Moses.

I think that's what she said.

Well, here I am again, years later.

I'm an old lady, now, as you can see.
But I'm no longer a slave.

None of us are. It was all down to my
baby brother, Moses.
Well, him and God.

It's sort of a long story ...

... but there was:

a burning bush

a meeting with Pharaoh

a bunch of plagues

a sea that split in two

and a defeated
Egyptian army.

Free to go to a new place God has promised us.

So I guess my little lullaby wasn't so silly, after all.

In fact, I'm just about to sing it to everyone. Here goes ...

I will sing to the Lord

For He has triumphed gloriously

The horse and his rider

He has thrown into the sea ...

The Lord is my strength and my song

And He has become my salvation!

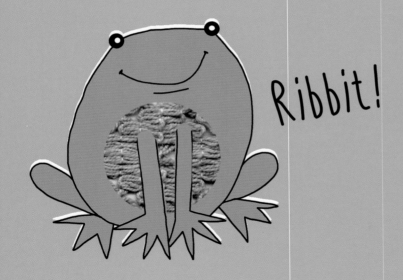

Ribbit!

Look out for another Talking Tale ...
YUMMM!! — Elijah, the boy and the amazing famine feast